Proverbs Study Guide
by Allison Jackson

Published by Walk with the Wise
Colorado Springs, CO 80923
United States

www.walkwiththewise.org
Email: walkwiththewiseone@gmail.com

Book cover and interior design by Allison Jackson.

ISBN 9798497635515

The Value of the Book of Proverbs

This Proverbs Study Guide can be used as a personal study, a family Bible study, a group study, or even a home-school course. It is designed to go through Proverbs chapter by chapter in the New King James version of the Bible.

To begin, read the chapter of Proverbs, and then answer the corresponding questions for that chapter. You will be amazed at how well you are able to retain the information after answering the questions!

In my family, we use this Proverbs Study Guide as a family devotional time. There's probably nothing I want more for my children than for them to appreciate and obtain the wisdom of God. We make this a special time where everybody curls up with blankets and we open the treasure chest of Proverbs. We keep it simple and fun. The Word of God is always life giving!

This study guide is a great conversation starter to discuss many of the issues that we all face in life. I have worked with a lot of young people. I've been a foster parent. I've had my own children. I've led groups of young people. The one thing I see that all young people are desperate for is WISDOM.

There is a generation today being raised without the teachings of wisdom, and they are starving for it. The majority of role models that exist right now for young people are not modeling wisdom or teaching it.

It is so vital that we learn wisdom for our own lives, and then pass it down to the next generation.

Say to wisdom, "You are my sister," And call understanding your nearest kin,
Proverbs 7:4 NKJV

Proverbs is like a never-ending well of wisdom and understanding. You can never exhaust the wisdom found in Proverbs. The benefits of wisdom are endless-including safety, honor, long life, good relationships, wealth and peace just to name a few. The more you read Proverbs, the more you will know the ways of God and the character of God.

Jesus is our wisdom. He is Proverbs personified!

The more you read, hear, and study the book of Proverbs, the more your ear will be tuned to discern the voice of wisdom versus the voice of folly.

Before you begin this study guide, ask the Lord for the Spirit of wisdom and revelation (Ephesians 1:17), that your spiritual eyes may be open to see and understand the wisdom found in the book of Proverbs.

It is important to understand that if you have received salvation, you have become a new creation (2 Corinthians 5:17), created in righteousness and true holiness (Ephesians 4:24). Therefore, all of the verses in Proverbs that talk about the righteous person are talking about you.

Wisdom will change your life forever!

Who Wrote the Book of Proverbs?

Proverbs 1-29 are written by Solomon, son of David, king of Israel (Proverbs 1:1). Proverbs 30-31 were added by Hezekiah's men when they copied out Solomon's proverbs (Proverbs 25:1).

1 Kings 4:32 says that Solomon spoke over 3,000 proverbs. Solomon also wrote the books of Ecclesiastes and Song of Solomon. According to the Bible, Solomon was the wisest man who ever lived; and the wisdom he had came directly from God. (1 Kings 3:12, 4:29-34; and 2 Chronicles 1:11-12).

God is the only true source of Heavenly wisdom.

What Is A Proverb?

A proverb is a concise saying that actually has much more meaning than meets the eye. A proverb may appear simple, but is tremendously deep and profound. This is why it is so necessary to read Proverbs with the Holy Spirit, Who leads us into all truth (John 16:13).

Ask the Holy Spirit to bring revelation of each proverb. The verses found in the book of Proverbs are God's wisdom. They are unchangeable truths that transcend time and culture.

Wisdom lies in front of every one of us "crying out loudly in the streets", longing to be noticed (Proverbs 1:20-23).

Proverbs Chapter 1

1. What does the book of Proverbs want us to perceive? vs. 2

_____

2. What does the book of Proverbs want us to receive? vs. 3

_____

3. What will Proverbs give to the young man? vs. 4

_____

4. Who attains wise counsel? vs. 5

_____

5. What do fools despise? vs. 7

_____

6. What is the beginning of knowledge? vs. 7

_____

7. What should you do if sinners entice you? vs. 10

_____

8. What happens to those greedy for gain? vs. 19

_____

9. Who hates knowledge? vs. 22

_____

10. What happens when you turn at the rebuke of wisdom? vs. 23

_____

11. What will destroy fools? vs. 32

_____

12. What happens to those who listen to wisdom? vs. 33

_____

Proverbs Chapter 2

1. What should you treasure within you? vs. 1

_____

2. What should you apply your heart to? vs. 2

_____

3. What should you incline your ear to? vs. 2

_____

4. What happens when you seek and search for wisdom? vs. 5

_____

5. Who gives wisdom? vs. 6

_____

6. Where do knowledge and understanding come from? vs. 6

_____

7. What does God store for the upright? vs. 7

_____

8. Who is God a shield for? vs. 7

_____

9. What paths are guarded by God? vs. 8

_____

10. Whose way does God preserve? vs. 8

_____

11. Where does wisdom enter? vs. 10

_____

12. What will preserve you? vs. 11

_____

13. What will keep you? vs. 11

_____

14. What will wisdom deliver you from? vs. 12

_____

15. Whose house leads down to death? vs. 16-18

_____

16. Who never regains the paths of life? vs. 19

_____

17. Who will be uprooted from the earth? vs. 22

_____

Proverbs Chapter 3

1.What should your heart keep? vs. 1

_____

2. What will keeping God's commands add to you? vs. 2

_____

3. How do you find favor in the sight of God and man? vs. 3-4

_____

4. What should you not lean on? vs. 5

_____

5. Who should you trust in with all your heart? vs. 5

_____

6. Is it good to be wise in your own eyes? vs. 7

_____

7. How do we depart from evil? vs. 7

_____

8. What will be health to your flesh and strength to your bones? vs. 7 -8

_____

9. How will a person's barns be filled with plenty? vs. 9-10

_____

10. Who does the Lord correct? vs. 12

_____

11. What is a key to happiness? vs. 13

_____

12. Whose proceeds are better than the profits of silver? vs. 13-14

_____

13. Who is better than anything you may desire? vs. 15

_____

14. What is in wisdom's right hand? vs. 16

_____

15. What are in wisdom's left hand? vs. 16

_____

16. What are all the paths of wisdom? vs. 17

_____

17. What is wisdom to those who take hold of her? vs. 18

_____

18. How did the Lord found the earth? vs. 19

_____

19. What will be life to your soul? vs. 21-22

_____

20. What should you not be afraid of? vs. 25

_____

21. Who is your confidence? vs. 26

_____

22. Why do neighbors live by a person? vs. 29

_____

23. Who does God give grace to? vs. 34

_____

24. What is the legacy of fools? vs. 35

_____

Proverbs Chapter 4

1.What should you give attention to? vs. 1

_____

2. What is the principal thing? vs. 7

_____

3. What should you get with wisdom? vs. 7

_____

4. What happens when you exalt wisdom? vs. 8

_____

5. What happens when you embrace wisdom? vs. 8

_____

6. What should a person take firm hold of? vs. 13

_____

7. What path should a person not enter? vs. 14

_____

8. Whose path gets brighter and brighter? vs. 18

_____

9. How is the way of the wicked like darkness? vs. 19

_____

10. List four things you should do with the Word. vs. 20-21

_____

11. What is health to all your flesh? vs. 20, 22

_____

12. What should you keep with all diligence? vs. 23

_____

13. Where do the issues of life spring from? vs. 23

_____

14. What should you put away from you? vs. 24

_____

15. What should be far from you? vs. 24

_____

Proverbs Chapter 5

1. What should you pay attention to? vs. 1

_____

2. What should you lend your ear to? vs. 1

_____

3. Whose lips drip honey? vs. 3

_____

4. Where do the immoral woman's feet lead to? vs. 5

_____

5. What should you not depart from? vs. 7

_____

6. What regrets does the sinful, dying man have? vs. 11-13

_____

7. Who should a man rejoice with? vs. 18

_____

8. What are before the eyes of the Lord? vs. 21

_____

9. What entraps the wicked man? vs. 22

_____

10. What is the wicked man caught in? vs. 22

_____

11. What causes the wicked man to die? vs. 23

_____

Proverbs Chapter 6

1. What are you snared by? vs. 2

_____

2. How is the ant wise? vs. 6-8

_____

3. Who walks with a perverse mouth? vs. 12

_____

4. What happens to a wicked man? vs. 15

_____

5. List two things that God hates. vs. 16-19

_____

6. What are the ways of life? vs. 23

_____

7. How is a man reduced to a crust of bread? vs. 26

_____

8. What happens when a thief is found? vs. 31

_____

9. What does a person who commits adultery lack? vs. 32

_____

10. Who destroys his own soul? vs. 32

_____

11. What does the man who commits adultery get? vs. 33

_____

Proverbs Chapter 7

1. What should you treasure within you? vs. 1

_____

2. What should you keep as the apple of your eye? vs. 2

_____

3. What should you say to wisdom? vs. 4

_____

4. Who should you call your nearest kin? vs. 4

_____

5. What will keep you from the immoral woman? vs. 4-5

_____

6. How does the seductress flatter people? vs. 5

_____

7. Who took the path to the harlot's house? vs. 7-8

_____

8. What was the young man devoid of? vs. 7

_____

9. How does the immoral woman cause people to yield to her? vs. 21

_____

10. How does the immoral woman seduce people? vs. 21

_____

11. Who is like an ox going to the slaughter? vs. 22

_____

12. What will cost a person their life? vs. 21-23

_____

13. Who is slain by the immoral woman? vs. 26

_____

14. Whose house is the way to hell? vs. 27

_____

Proverbs Chapter 8

1. Who lifts up her voice? vs.1

_____

2. Where does wisdom take her stand? vs. 2

_____

3. What will the mouth of wisdom speak? vs. 7

_____

4. Is there anything crooked or perverse in wisdom's words? vs. 8

_____

5. What is better to receive than silver? vs. 10

_____

6. What is better than choice gold? vs. 10

_____

7. What is better than rubies? vs. 11

_____

8.. What is the fear of the Lord? vs. 13

_____

9. What do kings use to reign? vs. 15

_____

10. Who lends to the Lord? vs. 17

_____

11. What happens to those who seek wisdom diligently? vs. 17

_____

12. What will happen to those who love wisdom? vs. 21

_____

13. What should we hear to be wise? vs 33

_____

14. Who obtains favor from the Lord? vs. 35

_____

15. Who wrongs his own soul and loves death? vs. 36

_____

Proverbs Chapter 9

1. What should we forsake to live? vs. 6

_____

2. What way should we go in? vs. 6

_____

3. What happens when you correct a scoffer? vs. 7-9

_____

4. What happens when you rebuke a wise man? vs. 8

_____

5. What happens when a wise man gets instruction? vs. 9

_____

6. What happens when you teach a just man? vs. 9

_____

7. What is the beginning of wisdom? vs. 10

_____

8. What is understanding? vs. 10

_____

9. What kind of woman is clamorous (loud, obnoxious, and boisterous)? vs. 13

_____

10. What does the foolish woman say to him who lacks understanding? vs. 17

_____

11. Where are the foolish woman's guests? vs. 18

_____

Proverbs Chapter 10

1. What is the grief of a mother? vs. 1

_____

2. What delivers from death? vs. 2

_____

3. What profits nothing? vs. 2

_____

4. What happens to a person with a slack hand? vs. 4

_____

5. What is on the head of the righteous? vs. 6

_____

6. Whose memory is blessed? vs. 7

_____

7. Who will receive commands? vs. 8

_____

8. What happens to those who don't walk in integrity? vs. 9

_____

9. Who walks securely? vs. 9

_____

10. What is a well of life? vs. 11

_____

11. What stirs up strife? vs. 12

_____

12. What covers all sins? vs. 12

_____)____

13. What do wise people store up? vs. 14

_____

14. What is a characteristic of the wise? vs. 19

_____

15. What is not lacking in a multitude of words? vs. 19

_____

16. Why do fools die? vs. 21

_____

17. What does the blessing of the Lord do? vs. 22

_____

18. What will come upon the wicked? vs. 24

_____

19. What will prolong your days? vs. 27

_____

20. Whose years will be shortened? vs. 27

_____

21. What does the mouth of the righteous bring forth? vs. 31

_____

Proverbs Chapter 11

1. What is an abomination to the Lord? vs 1

_____

2. What is a delight to the Lord? vs. 1

_____

3. What comes after pride? vs. 2

_____

4. What will guide the upright? vs. 3

_____

5. What is the righteous delivered from? vs. 8

_____

6. Where does trouble go? vs. 8

_____

7. How are the righteous delivered? vs. 9

_____

8. What happens when it goes well with the righteous? vs. 10

_____

9. How is a city exalted? vs. 11

_____

10. Who despises his neighbor? vs. 12

_____

11. Who holds his peace? vs. 12

_____

12. What happens where there is no counsel? vs. 14

_____

13. Who retains honor? vs. 16

_____

14. Who does good for his own soul? vs. 17

_____

15. Who troubles his own flesh? vs. 17

_____

16. Who does deceptive work? vs. 18

_____

17. What happens to the person who sows righteousness? vs. 18

_____

18. What leads to life? vs. 19

_____

19. What is like a ring of gold in a swine's snout? vs. 22

_____

20. What happens when you withhold more than what is right? vs. 24

_____

21. What kind of soul will be made rich? vs. 25

_____

22. What happens to a person who trusts in their riches? vs. 28

_____

23. Who will the fool be a servant to? vs. 29

_____

24. Who is wise? vs. 30

_____

Proverbs Chapter 12

1. Who is stupid? vs. 1

_____

2. Who obtains God's favor? vs. 2

_____

3. What is like rottenness in a man's bones? vs. 4

_____

4. What delivers the upright? vs. 6

_____

5. What happens to the house of the righteous? vs. 7

_____

6. Who regards the life of his animal? vs. 10

_____

7. Who will be satisfied with bread? vs. 11

_____

8. Who will come through trouble? vs. 13

_____

9. How will a man be satisfied with good? vs. 14

_____

10. What is a characteristic of the wise? vs. 15

_____

11. What does the tongue of the wise promote? vs. 18

_____

12. Who has joy? vs. 20

_____

13. What will not overtake the righteous? vs. 21

_____

14. Who are a delight to the Lord? vs. 22

_____

15. What is an abomination to the Lord? vs. 22

_____

16. Whose hand will rule? vs. 24

_____

17. What causes depression? vs. 25

_____

18. Why should the righteous choose their friends carefully? vs. 26

_____

19. What is man's precious possession? vs. 27

_____

20. In what pathway is there no death? vs. 28

_____

Proverbs Chapter 13

1. How does a person preserve his life? vs. 3

_____

2. Who shall have destruction? vs. 3

_____

3. What happens to the soul of a lazy man? vs. 4

_____

4. What happens to the soul of the diligent? vs. 4

_____

5. What does a righteous man hate? vs. 5

_____

6. Where does strife come from? vs. 10

_____

7. What happens to wealth gained by dishonesty? vs. 11

_____

8. Who will increase? vs. 11

_____

9. What makes the heart sick? vs. 12

_____

10. What happens to someone who despises the Word? vs. 13

_____

11. Who is rewarded? vs. 13

_____

12. What gains favor? vs. 15

_____

13. Whose way is hard? vs 15

_____

14. What comes to those who disdain correction? vs. 18

_____

15. Who will be honored? vs. 18

_____

16. What is sweet to the soul? vs. 19

_____

17. What happens to someone who walks with wise men? vs. 20

_____

18. What happens to a companion of fools? vs. 20

_____

19. Who does evil pursue? vs. 21

_____

20. Who is good repaid to? vs. 21

_____

21. What is stored up for the righteous? vs. 22

_____

22. Who does a good man leave an inheritance to? vs. 22

_____

23. Who hates his son? vs. 24

_____

24. What does the person who loves his son do? vs. 24

_____

Proverbs Chapter 14

1. What does the wise woman build?

_____

2. Who fears the Lord? vs. 2

_____

3. Who despises the Lord? vs. 2

_____

4. What is in the mouth of a fool? vs. 3

_____

5. What will preserve the wise? vs. 3

_____

6. Who seeks wisdom and does not find it? vs. 6

_____

7. What should you do when you don't perceive in man the lips of knowledge? vs. 7

_____

8. Who mocks at sin? vs. 9

_____

9. What happens to the tent of the righteous? vs. 11

_____

10. What is the end of the way that seems right to man? vs. 12

_____

11. Who will be satisfied from above? vs. 14

_____

12. Who believes everything people say? vs. 15

_____

13. Who considers well his steps? vs. 15

_____

14. Who fears and departs from evil? vs. 16

_____

15. Who acts foolishly? vs. 17

_____

16. Who is hated? vs. 17

_____

17. What do the simple inherit? vs. 18

_____

18. Who will bow before the good? vs. 19

_____

19. Is it sin to despise your neighbor? vs. 21

_____

20. What happens to the man who has mercy on the poor? vs. 21

_____

21. What is the crown of the wise? vs. 24

_____

22. Where is there strong confidence? vs. 26

_____

23. Who has great understanding? vs. 29

_____

24. Who exalts folly? vs. 29

_____

25. What is life to the body? vs. 30

_____

26. What is rottenness to the bones? vs. 30

_____

27. What does a person who honors the Lord do? vs. 31

_____

28. What exalts a nation? vs. 34

_____

Proverbs Chapter 15

1.What stirs up anger? vs. 1

_____

2. What turns away wrath? vs. 1

_____

3. Where are the eyes of the Lord? vs. 3

_____

4. What is a tree of life? vs. 4

_____

5. What breaks the spirit? vs. 4

_____

6. What does a fool despise? vs. 5

_____

7. What is a characteristic of the prudent? vs. 5

_____

8. Where is there much treasure? vs. 6

_____

9. What do the lips of the wise disperse? vs. 7

_____

10. What is a delight to the Lord? vs. 8

_____

11. Who is harsh discipline for? vs. 10

_____

12. What happens to a person who hates correction? vs. 10

_____

13. What makes a cheerful countenance? vs. 13

_____

14. What does sorrow of the heart do to the spirit? vs. 13

_____

15. What does the heart of the person with understanding seek? vs. 14

_____

16. Who has a continual feast? vs. 15

_____

17. What is the way of the lazy man like? vs. 19

_____

18. What is the way of the upright like? vs. 19

_____

19. Who enjoys folly? vs. 21

_____

20. When do plans go awry? vs. 22

_____

21. Whose way of life winds upward? vs. 24

_____

22. Who troubles his own house? vs. 27

_____

23. What does the heart of the righteous do? vs. 28

_____

24. What makes your bones healthy? vs. 30

_____

25. Who will abide among the wise? vs. 31

_____

26. Who despises his own soul? vs. 32

_____

27. What happens to a person who heeds rebuke? vs. 32

_____

28. What is the fear of the Lord? vs. 33

_____

29. What is before honor? vs. 33

_____

Proverbs Chapter 16

1. What happens when you commit your works to the Lord? vs. 3

_____

2. Who is an abomination to the Lord? vs. 5

_____

3. How does a person depart from evil? vs. 6

_____

4. What happens when a man's ways please the Lord? vs. 7

_____

5. What plans a man's way? vs. 9

_____

6. What is better than getting gold? vs. 16

_____

7. What is the highway of the upright? vs. 17

_____

8. How can you preserve your soul? vs. 17

_____

9. What comes before destruction? vs. 18

_____

10. What comes before a fall? vs. 18

_____

11. Who will find good? vs. 20

_____

12. Who is happy? vs. 20

_____

13. What increases learning? vs. 21

_____

14. What is a wellspring of life? vs. 22

_____

15. What is health to the bones? vs. 24

_____

16. What does an ungodly man do? vs. 27

_____

17. Who sows strife? vs. 28

_____

18. Who is better than the mighty? vs. 32

_____

Proverbs Chapter 17

1. Who tests the hearts? vs. 3

_____

2. Who reproaches his Maker? vs. 5

_____

3. Who are the crown of old men? vs. 6

_____

4. Who is the glory of children? vs. 6

_____

5. Who seeks love? vs. 9

_____

6. Who seperates friends? vs. 9

_____

7. What is more effective than a hundred blows on a fool? vs. 10

_____

8. What happens to an evil man who seeks rebellion? vs. 11

_____

9. What are two abominations to the Lord? vs. 15

_____

10. Who shakes hands in a pledge and becomes surety for his friend? vs. 18

_____

11. What happens to someone with a perverse tongue? vs. 20

_____

12. What dries the bones? vs. 22

_____

13. What does good like medicine? vs. 22

_____

14. Who accepts a bribe? vs. 23

_____

15. Who spares his words? vs. 27

_____

16. Who has a calm spirit? vs. 27

_____

17. When is even a fool counted wise? vs. 28

_____

Proverbs Chapter 18

1. Who rages against all wise judgment? vs. 1

_____

2. What does a fool want to express? vs. 2

_____

3. What does a fool have no delight in? vs. 2

_____

4. What is a fool's destruction? vs. 7

_____

5. Who is the brother of a great destroyer? vs. 9

_____

6. Where do the righteous run for safety? vs. 10

_____

7. What happens before destruction? vs. 12

_____

8. Is it good to answer a matter before you hear it? vs. 13

_____

9. What will sustain a man in sickness? vs. 14

_____

10. What does the ear of the wise seek? vs. 15

_____

11. What will bring a person before great men? vs. 16

_____

12. What are like the bars of a castle? vs. 19

_____

13. What is in the power of the tongue? vs. 21

_____

14. Who finds a good thing and obtains favor from the Lord? vs. 22

_____

Proverbs Chapter 19

1. Who is better than one perverse in his lips? vs. 1

_____

2. What is not good for your soul? vs. 2

_____

3. What twists a man's way? vs. 3

_____

4. What makes many friends? vs. 4

_____

5. Who loves his own soul? vs. 8

_____

6. Who will find good? vs. 8

_____

7. Who will not go unpunished? vs. 5, 9

_____

8. What is not fitting for a fool? vs. 10

_____

9. What makes a man slow to anger? vs. 11

_____

10. What is a man's glory? vs. 11

_____

11. Where does a prudent wife come from? vs. 14

_____

12. What happens to an idle person? vs. 15

_____

13. Who lends to the Lord? vs. 17

_____

14. What will cause you to be wise in your latter days? vs. 20

_____

15. What is desired in a man? vs. 22

_____

16. Who will abide in satisfaction and not be visited with evil? vs. 23

_____

17. What happens when you rebuke one who has understanding? vs. 25

_____

18. How does a person stray from the words of knowledge? vs. 27

_____

Proverbs Chapter 20

1. Who is not wise? vs. 1

_____

2. What is honorable for a man? vs. 3

_____

3. What happens to the lazy man during harvest? vs. 4

_____

4. What does a righteous man walk in? vs. 7

_____

5. Whose children are blessed? vs. 7

_____

6. What happens if you love sleep? vs. 13

_____

7. What is a precious jewel? vs. 15

_____

8. What happens after bread is gained by deceit? vs. 17

_____

9. How are plans established? vs. 18

_____

10. Who should you not associate with? vs. 19

_____

11. Whose lamp will be put out in deep darkness? vs. 20

_____

12. What happens to an inheritance gained hastily? vs. 21

_____

13. What should you do instead of recompensing evil? vs. 22

_____

14. What is the lamp of the Lord? vs. 27

_____

Proverbs Chapter 21

1. Where is the king's heart? vs. 1

_____

2. What is more acceptable to the Lord than sacrifice? vs. 3

_____

3. Is it good to have a proud heart? vs. 4

_____

4. Where do the plans of the diligent lead? vs.5

_____

5. Where do the plans of the hasty lead? vs. 5

_____

6. Whose way is perverse? vs. 8

_____

7. What does the soul of the wicked desire? vs. 10

_____

8. Who does God overthrow? vs. 12

_____

9. Should we shut our ears to the cry of the poor? vs. 13

_____

10. Who does destruction come to? vs. 15

_____

11. What happens to the person who wanders from the way of understanding? vs. 16

_____

12. Who is guaranteed to be a poor man? vs. 17

_____

13. It is better to dwell in the wilderness than with who? vs. 19

_____

14. How does a person keep their soul from troubles? vs. 23

_____

15. Whose hands refuse to labor? vs. 25

_____

16. What does the lazy man do all day long? vs. 26

_____

17. Who gives and does not spare? vs. 26

_____

18. Is there any wisdom against the Lord? vs. 30

_____

19. Where does deliverance come from? vs. 31

_____

Proverbs Chapter 22

1.What is better than great riches? vs. 1

_____

2. What do the rich and poor have in common? vs. 2

_____

3. What brings riches, honor, and life? vs. 4

_____

4. Who is a servant to the lender? vs. 7

_____

5. How do you reap sorrow? vs. 8

_____

6. Who will be blessed? vs. 9

_____

7. What happens when you cast out a scoffer? vs. 10

_____

8. What do the eyes of the Lord preserve? vs. 12

_____

9. What happens to the words of the faithless? vs. 12

_____

10. What excuse does the lazy man make? vs. 13

_____

11. What is a deep pit? vs. 14

_____

12. What is bound up in the heart of a child? vs. 15

_____

13. What will drive foolishness from a child? vs. 15

_____

14. What happens to the person who oppresses the poor to increase his riches? vs. 16

_____

15. What should you incline your ear to and hear? vs. 17

_____

16. Who pleads the cause of the poor and afflicted? vs. 22-23

_____

17. Who should a person not be friends with? vs. 24

_____

18. What happens when you learn the ways of an angry man? vs. 25

_____

19. Is it wise to be surety for another person's debt? vs. 26

_____

20. What happens to a man who excels in his work? vs. 29

_____

Proverbs Chapter 23

1. Should you overwork to be rich? vs. 4

_____

2. What flies away like an eagle toward heaven? vs. 5

_____

3. Why should you not speak in the hearing of a fool? vs. 9

_____

4. What should you apply your heart to? vs. 12

_____

5. What should you apply your ear to? vs. 12

_____

6. Who should you not withhold correction from? vs. 13

_____

7. What happens when you beat a child with a rod? vs. 14

_____

8. What should we be zealous for? vs. 17

_____

9. What are you supposed to guide? vs. 19

_____

10. What happens to the glutton and drunkard? vs. 21

_____

11. What is a drowsy man clothed with? vs. 21

_____

12. List six things that come with drinking too much wine. vs. 29-30

_____

13. What bites like a serpent and stings like a viper? vs. 31, 32

_____

14. What does your heart utter when you've had too much to drink? vs. 33

_____

Proverbs Chapter 24

1.Who should you not desire to be with? vs. 1

_____

2. Who is strong? vs. 5

_____

3. Who increases strength? vs. 5

_____

4. Where is there safety? vs. 6

_____

5. What is too lofty for a fool? vs. 7

_____

6. What does it mean if you faint in the day of adversity? vs. 10

_____

7. Who are we instructed to deliver? vs. 11

_____

8. What is like honey to your soul? vs. 13-14

_____

9. What happens to the righteous man who falls seven times? vs. 16

_____

10. Who should we not associate with? vs. 21

_____

11. Who will the people curse? vs. 24

_____

12. What happens to those who rebuke the wicked? vs. 25

_____

13. What is a lazy man devoid of? vs. 30

_____

14. What can we learn from the field of a lazy man? vs 30-34

_____

Proverbs Chapter 25

1. What is the glory of kings? vs. 1

_____

2. Should you exalt yourself in the presence of a king? vs. 6

_____

3. Where should we not go hastily? vs. 8

_____

4. Who is like clouds and wind without rain? vs. 14

_____

5. What happens if you eat too much honey? vs. 16

_____

6. Why should a person seldom set foot in their neighbor's house? vs. 17

_____

7. What is like a broken tooth and dislocated foot? vs. 19

_____

8. Should we sing songs to a heavy heart? vs. 20

_____

9. What happens when a person gives food and water to their enemy? vs. 21-22

_____

10. What brings an angry countenance? vs. 23

_____

11. What is like a murky spring and a polluted well? vs. 26

_____

12. Should we seek our own glory? vs. 27

_____

13. Who is like a city broken down, without walls? vs. 28

_____

Proverbs Chapter 26

1. What is not fitting for a fool? vs. 1

_____

2. What happens when you answer a fool according to his folly? vs. 4-5

_____

3. What is like the legs of the lame that hang limp? vs. 7

_____

4. Who is like a dog returning to his own vomit? vs. 11

_____

5. Is it good to be wise in your own eyes? vs. 12

_____

6. What is like a door turning on its hinges? vs. 14

_____

7. Who is like a person who takes a dog by the ears? vs. 17

_____

8. Who is like a firebrand, arrow, and death-throwing mad man? vs. 18, 19

_____

9. Where does strife cease? vs. 20

_____

10. Who kindles strife? vs. 21

_____

11. Where do the words of a talebearer go? vs. 22

_____

12. What happens to the person who hides hate in his heart? vs. 24-26

_____

13. What does it mean when a person lies? vs. 28

_____

14. What works ruin? vs. 28

_____

Proverbs Chapter 27

1.Why should you not boast about tomorrow? vs. 1

_____

2. Whose mouth should praise you? vs. 2

_____

3. What is heavier than sand and stone? vs. 3

_____

4. What is better than love carefully concealed? vs. 5

_____

5. What are deceitful? vs. 6

_____

6. What is sweet to a hungry soul? vs. 7

_____

7. What happens to those who ignore evil? vs. 12

_____

8. Who foresees evil and hides himself? vs. 12

_____

9. What is like restraining the wind or grasping oil? vs 15-16

_____

10.What does a man sharpen? vs. 17

_____

11. What reveals a man like a reflection in water? vs. 19

_____

12. What are never satisfied? vs. 20

_____

13. What are not forever? vs. 24

_____

Proverbs Chapter 28

1. Who are as bold as a lion? vs. 1

_____

2. Who flees when no one pursues? vs. 1

_____

3. Who is like a driving rain that leaves no food? vs. 3

_____

4. Who praises the wicked? vs. 4

_____

5. What do evil men not understand? vs. 5

_____

6. A person who increases their possessions by usury and extortion gathers it for who? vs. 8

_____

7. Whose prayer is an abomination? vs. 9

_____

8. Who will fall into his own pit? vs. 10

_____

9. What happens to a man who covers his sins? vs. 13

_____

10. What does a person receive when they confess and forsake their sin? vs. 13

_____

11. A person who is always reverent is what? vs. 14

_____

12. What happens to the person who hardens his heart? vs. 14

_____

13. Who will abound with blessings? vs. 20

_____

14. Who hastens after riches? vs. 22

_____

15. Who is a companion to a destroyer? vs. 24

_____

16. Who will not lack? vs. 27

_____

Proverbs Chapter 29

1. Who will suddenly be destroyed? vs. 1

_____

2. What happens when a wicked man rules? vs. 2

_____

3. What happens when the righteous are in authority? vs. 2

_____

4. Who makes his father rejoice? vs. 3

_____

5. Who vents all his feelings? vs. 11

_____

6. Who holds back his feelings? vs. 11

_____

7. What give wisdom to a child? vs. 15

_____

8. What brings shame to a mother? vs. 15

_____

9. What happens when you correct your child? vs. 17

_____

10. What happens when there is no revelation? vs. 18

_____

11. Who is worse off than a fool? vs. 20

_____

12. Who stirs up strife? vs. 22

_____

13. Who abounds in transgression? vs. 22

_____

14. What will bring a man low? vs 23

_____

15. Who will retain honor? vs 23

_____

16. Who hates his own life? vs. 24

_____

17. What does the fear of man bring? vs. 25

_____

18. Who will be safe? vs. 25

_____

19. Where does justice for man come from? vs. 26

_____

Proverbs Chapter 30

1.Who is God a shield to? vs. 5

_____

2. Whose words are pure? vs. 5

_____

3. What should we not add to? vs. 6

_____

4. Should we slander a worker to their employer? vs. 10

_____

5. What is true about the generation that's pure in its own eyes? vs. 12

_____

6. What are four things that never say "enough"? vs. 15-16

_____

7. What does the adulterous woman say? vs. 20

_____

8. What four things are little but wise? vs. 24-28

_____

9. Is it foolish or wise to exalt yourself? vs. 32

_____

10. What should a person do if they have devised evil? vs. 32

_____

Proverbs Chapter 31

1.Who is wine not for? vs. 4

_____

2. Who should we open our mouth for? vs. 8

_____

3. Whose worth is far above rubies? vs. 10

_____

4. Who will have no lack of gain? vs. 11

_____

5. What does the virtuous wife gird herself with? vs. 17

_____

6. Who does the virtuous wife extend her hand to? vs. 20

_____

7. What is on a virtuous wife's tongue? vs. 26

_____

8. What is passing? vs. 30

_____

9. What is deceitful? vs. 30

_____

10. What kind of woman will be praised? vs. 30

_____

Made in the USA
Las Vegas, NV
28 October 2024

10649721R00050